W9-BXL-123

READING POWER

Extreme Machines

Big Rigs

Scott P. Werther

The Rosen Publishing Group's
PowerKids Press™
New York

Published in 2002 by The Rosen Publishing Group, Inc.
29 East 21st Street, New York, NY 10010

First Edition

Book Design: Michelle Innes

Photo Credits: Cover, pp. 4–5, 8–9, 11, 13, 14–15, 17, 19 © Mike Campbell; pp. 6–7 © Wayne Aldridge/International Stock; p. 21 © Photodisc

Werther, Scott P.
Big rigs / Scott P. Werther.
    p. cm. – (Extreme machines)
Includes bibliographical references and index.
ISBN 0-8239-5956-2 (library binding)
1. Tractor trailer combinations–Juvenile literature. [1. Tractor trailers. 2. Trucks.] I. Title.
TL230.15 .W47 2001
629.224–dc21

                                        2001000158

Manufactured in the United States of America

Contents

A Big Rig

This is a big rig.
It is a long truck.

This big rig weighs more than 13 tons.

This big rig has 18 wheels.
It also has strong brakes.

9

This big rig has many lights.
These lights help the driver to
drive at night.

This is the diesel engine of a big rig. Diesel engines help big rigs carry heavy loads.

The Trailer and Cab

A big rig has a trailer and a cab.

trailer

cab

The driver's seat is in the cab.

17

Some cabs have small beds.
The driver can sleep here
during long trips.

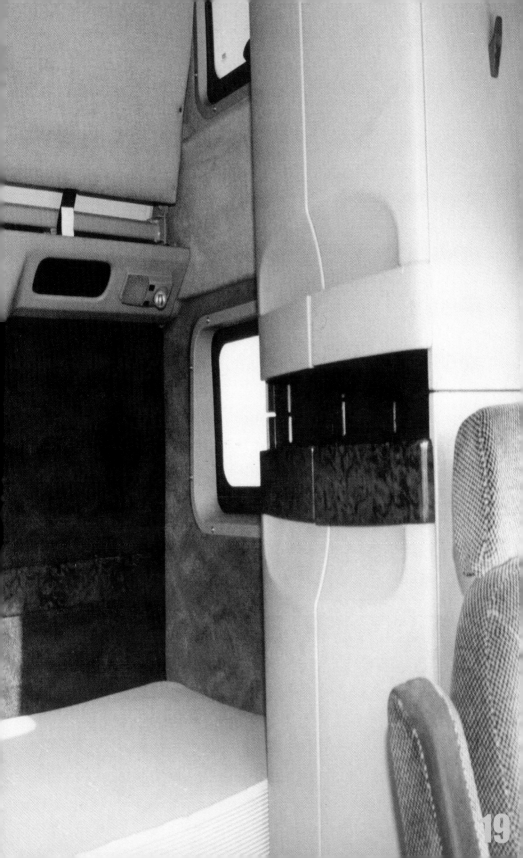

Across the Country

Big rigs travel thousands of miles each year across the country. They carry things we buy in stores, such as food and clothes.

Glossary

big rig (**bihg rihg**) a long truck that has a trailer and a cab

brakes (**brayks**) devices that press against the wheels to slow or stop a vehicle

cab (**kab**) the short front part of a big rig where the driver sits

diesel (**dee**-zuhl) an engine that burns oil with heat produced by compressing air

engine (**ehn**-juhn) the part of a truck that gives it power

trailer (**tray**-luhr) the back part of a big rig

Resources

Books

Mighty Machines: Big Rig
by Caroline Bingham, Mary Ling, and
Deni Brown
Dorling Kindersley Publishing (1996)

The Big Book of Trucks
by Caroline Bingham
Dorling Kindersley Publishing (1999)

Web Site
Big Rigs
http://corvettegold.com/bigrigs.htm

Index

Word Count: 113

Note to Librarians, Teachers, and Parents

If reading is a challenge, Reading Power is a solution! Reading Power is perfect for readers who want high-interest subject matter at an accessible reading level. These fact-filled, photo-illustrated books are designed for readers who want straightforward vocabulary, engaging topics, and a manageable reading experience. With clear picture/text correspondence, leveled Reading Power books put the reader in charge. Now readers have the power to get the information they want and the skills they need in a user-friendly format.